SUPERDOODLES

SPORTS

WRITTEN AND ILLUSTRATED BY BEV ARMSTRONG

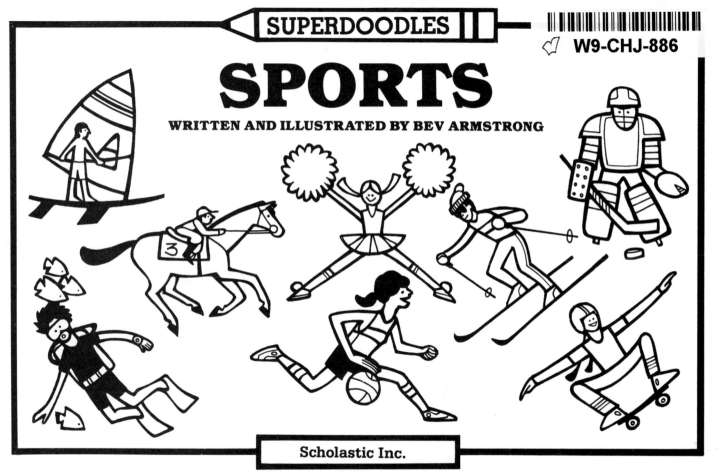

Scholastic Inc.

New York   Toronto   London   Auckland   Sydney

ISBN 0-590-99646-0

Designed and edited by Sherri M. Butterfield. Copyright © 1993 by The Learning Works, Inc. All rights reserved. Published by Scholastic Inc., 555 Broadway, New York, NY 10012, by arrangement with The Learning Works, Inc.

12 11 10 9 8 7 6 5 4 3 2 1   6 7 8 9/9 0 1/0

Printed in the U.S.A.   08

First Scholastic printing, September 1996

Introduction

SUPERDOODLES are books that provide simple, step-by-step instructions for super line drawings. The figures in this book may be sketched large for murals or posters, or small for bookmarks and flip books. They may be used individually in separate pictures or combined in various positions to create an action-packed sports scene.

As you follow the steps, draw in pencil. Dotted lines appear in some steps. Make these lines light so that they can be easily erased later. When you have finished your drawing, erase all unnecessary lines. To give your drawing a finished look, go over the remaining lines with a colored pencil, crayon, or felt-tipped pen.

If you enjoy this book, look for other **Learning Works SUPERDOODLES.** Titles in this series include *Dinosaurs, Mammals, Rain Forest,* and *Vehicles.*

baseball player

Make a picture that includes both this pitcher and the batter on page 4.

3

baseball player

Give your player a uniform like that of your favorite baseball team.

basketball player

Just for fun, draw roller skates on the basketball player.

basketball player

Add a basket and a backboard to your drawing.

cheerleader

Draw a group of leaping cheerleaders. Dress them in your school colors.

diver

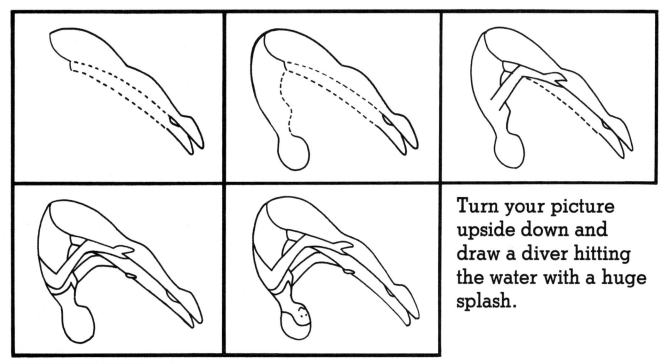

Turn your picture upside down and draw a diver hitting the water with a huge splash.

figure skater

Draw your skater on a large rink or frozen pond. Make lines on the ice to show where she has skated.

football player

Draw a jumping cheerleader on each side of your football player. See page 7.

football player

Using this drawing, make a poster for a football game. Include the names of the teams that will play.

gymnast

Redraw your gymnast with both legs pointing straight up.

gymnast

In this shape, design a leotard for an Olympic gymnast.

hang glider

Add a sun, clouds, and birds to your picture. Is the hang glider flying over water, fields, or a forest?

high jumper

Create a cartoon of someone jumping over a fence to get away from a snake, an alligator, a lion, or some other animal.

hockey player

Make a drawing that includes this hockey player and the goalie on page 17.

hockey player

On a large piece of paper or poster board, draw a BIG picture of a tough-looking goalie.

jockey

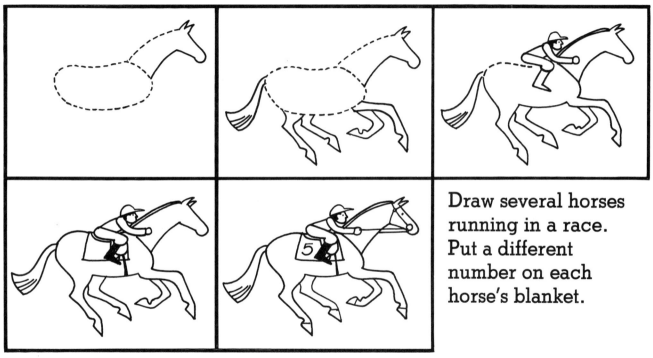

Draw several horses running in a race. Put a different number on each horse's blanket.

long jumper

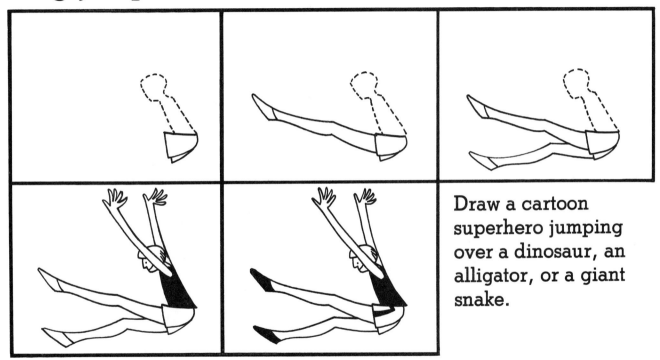

Draw a cartoon superhero jumping over a dinosaur, an alligator, or a giant snake.

pole vaulter

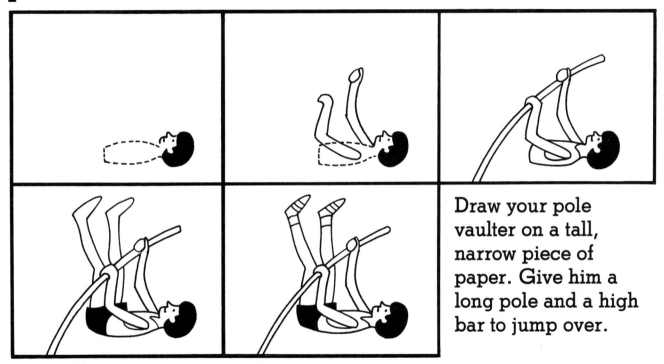

Draw your pole vaulter on a tall, narrow piece of paper. Give him a long pole and a high bar to jump over.

roller skater

Give your skater a kite to fly or draw a dog running beside her.

rope jumper

Draw a person who is jumping rope while bouncing on a trampoline.

scuba diver

Draw fishes, seals, turtles, and/or other sea animals around your scuba diver.

skateboarder

Draw a skateboarder zooming down a ramp or over an obstacle.

skier

Draw a skier sliding down a long snowy slope—or flying through the air!

25

soccer player

Put your favorite number on this girl's shirt and dress her in your favorite colors.

speed skater

Draw a row of speed skaters competing in a race.

surfer

Give your surfer a *huge* wave. Add a sun and clouds to your picture.

tennis player

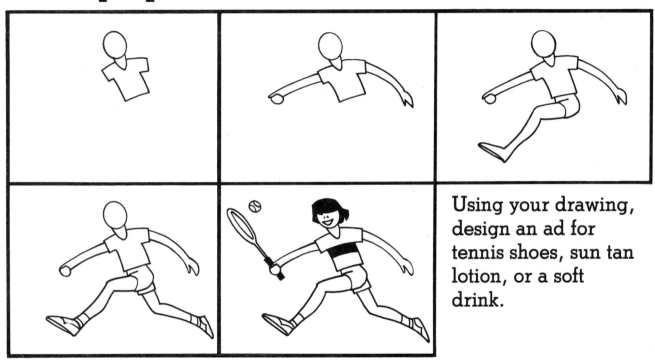

Using your drawing, design an ad for tennis shoes, sun tan lotion, or a soft drink.

volleyball player

Add other volleyball players and a net to your drawing.

weight lifter

Just for fun, draw a weight lifter holding a huge toothbrush, a bone, a hot dog, a pencil, or a candy cane.

windsurfer

Draw several windsurfers sailing on the ocean on a bright sunny day.